Dedicated to my friend Wayan Sukerta. Wayan was sixteen when I first met him, a farmer's son who was studying English so he could work in tourism. Over the years, we have spent many hours talking in English and walking in sawahs. When I decided to do this book, I rode on the back of Wayan's motorcycle from sawah to sawah, looking for animals and learning from him about how rice grows. My most adventurous sawah experience with Wayan was when we went "eeling" in the middle of the night with a lantern, a pail, and a plierlike tool for snatching eels. But we didn't catch very many eels because Wayan was mostly occupied with saving me from falling into the mud. He is now a certified tour guide and his English is terrific. Thank you, Wayan, for teaching me about life in the sawah.

—R.G.G.

For my friends Junsun and Sanghee

—Y.C.

Henry Holt and Company, LLC, *Publishers since 1866*
115 West 18th Street, New York, New York 10011

Henry Holt is a registered trademark
of Henry Holt and Company, LLC

Published in Canada by Fitzhenry & Whiteside Ltd.,
195 Allstate Parkway, Markham, Ontario L3R 4T8.

Library of Congress Cataloging-in-Publication Data
Gelman, Rita Golden.
Rice is life / Rita Golden Gelman; paintings by Yangsook Choi.
Summary: Text and illustrations demonstrate the importance of rice to life
on the island of Bali in the country of Indonesia, where rice is consumed
for breakfast, lunch, and dinner.
1. Rice—Indonesia—Bali Island—Juvenile literature.   2. Riceland animals—
Indonesia—Bali Island—Juvenile literature.   [1. Rice.   2. Bali Island
(Indonesia)—Social life and customs.]   I. Choi, Yangsook, ill.   II. Title.
SB191.R5G424   1999   633.1'8'095986—dc21   98-34055

ISBN 0-8050-5719-6 / First Edition—2000
The artist used oil on paper to create the illustrations for this book.
Printed in the United States of America on acid-free paper. ∞

10 9 8 7 6 5 4 3 2 1

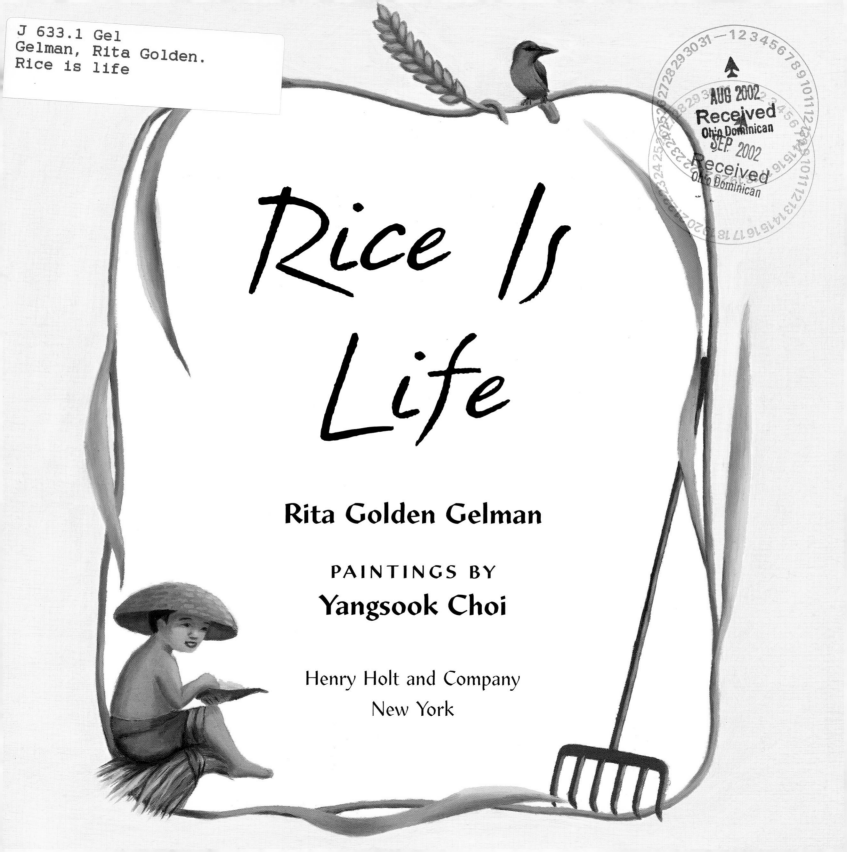

Rice Is Life

Rita Golden Gelman

PAINTINGS BY
Yangsook Choi

Henry Holt and Company
New York

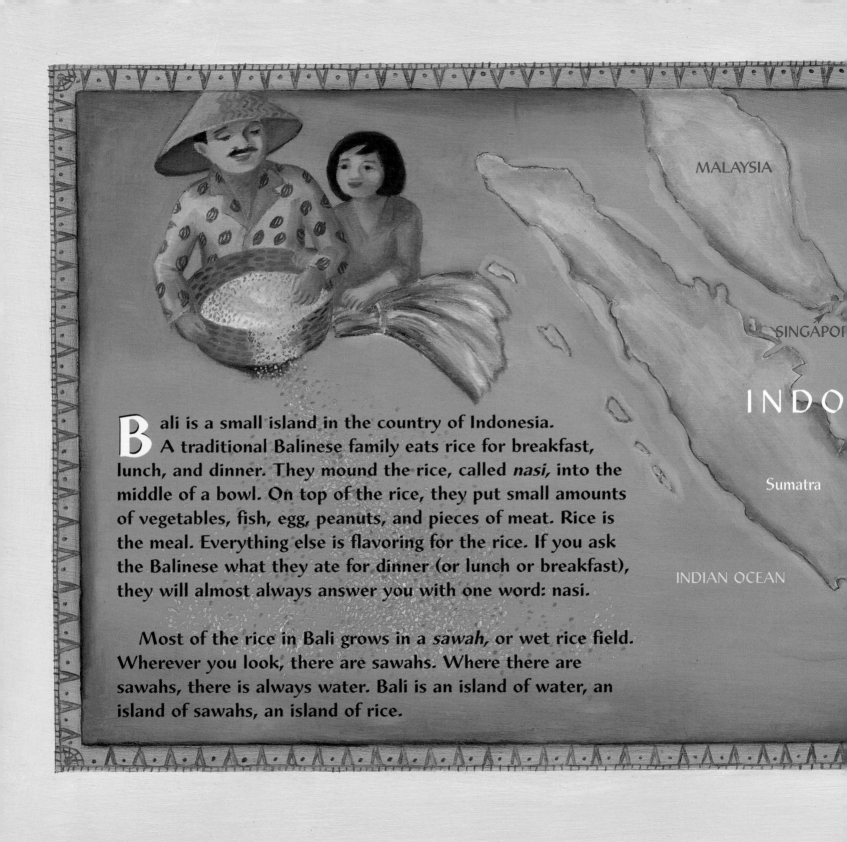

Bali is a small island in the country of Indonesia. A traditional Balinese family eats rice for breakfast, lunch, and dinner. They mound the rice, called *nasi,* into the middle of a bowl. On top of the rice, they put small amounts of vegetables, fish, egg, peanuts, and pieces of meat. Rice is the meal. Everything else is flavoring for the rice. If you ask the Balinese what they ate for dinner (or lunch or breakfast), they will almost always answer you with one word: nasi.

Most of the rice in Bali grows in a *sawah,* or wet rice field. Wherever you look, there are sawahs. Where there are sawahs, there is always water. Bali is an island of water, an island of sawahs, an island of rice.

SOUTH CHINA SEA

BRUNEI

MALAYSIA

B O R N E O

Kalimantan

NESIA*

JAVA SEA

Java

Bali

* Indonesia comprises Bali, Java, Kalimantan, and Sumatra.

In the wet and fertile sawah,
Where the mud is warm and deep,
Small and slippery eels live.
They swim.
They eat.
They sleep.
The egrets come to get them,
Picking,
Poking for their prey,
While the slippery little eels
Try to quickly
Slip away
Through the sawah,
Where the mud is warm and deep.

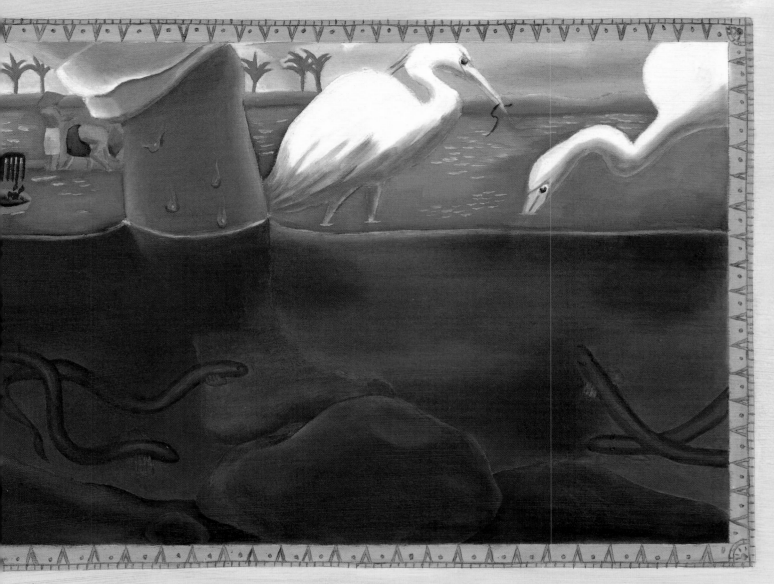

The farmers are getting ready to plant. They are cleaning the irrigation ditches, patching up the sides of the sawah, and packing mud where rain has washed away the paths.

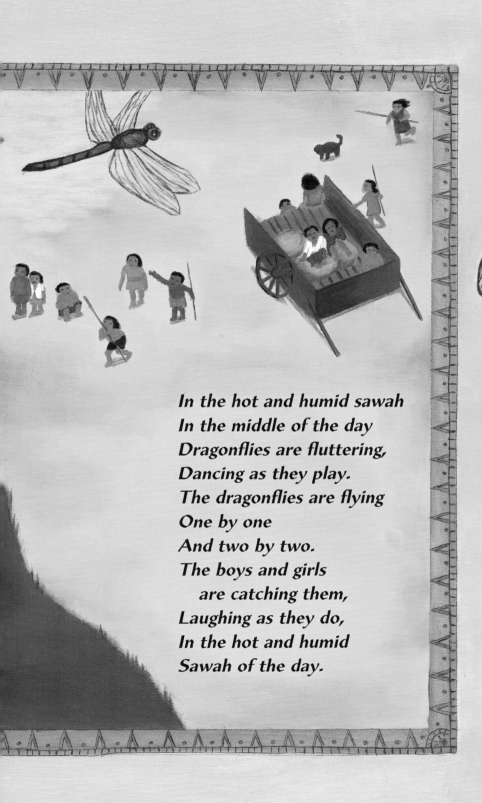

In the hot and humid sawah
In the middle of the day
Dragonflies are fluttering,
Dancing as they play.
The dragonflies are flying
One by one
And two by two.
The boys and girls
* are catching them,*
Laughing as they do,
In the hot and humid
Sawah of the day.

The boys and girls are "fishing" for dragonflies with poles tipped with sap. When the dragonflies touch the sap, they stick. The children remove the wings and put the insects, still wriggling, onto a bamboo skewer. Later, the children will cook them over a fire. In Bali, dragonflies are tasty snacks.

As the sun sets in the sawah,
And the sky is purple-red,
A child and his mother watch
While bats fly overhead.
Bats are looking for mosquitoes.
They are eating as they fly.
Flapping,
Darting,
Swooping,
Moving pictures in the sky
Above the sawah,
When the sky
Is purple-red.

The rice plants in their seed beds are big enough to be planted in the fields. The farmer lifts out a handful of seedlings and places them on a tray. When the tray is filled, he begins planting.

In the gray and dreary sawah
Where the wind and rain
    are stinging,
There's a black and leggy spider
Big and sprawly,
Bravely clinging.
Pounded by the water,
Staring straight ahead,
The patient leggy spider sits
Swinging on its thread,
In the sawah
Where the rain and wind
Are stinging.

The plants are nourished by water from the mountains and the sky. The tubelike center stem begins to bulge. Each day the bulge grows fatter. When the plants reach this stage, the Balinese say, "The rice plant is pregnant."

In the darkness of the sawah
With a yellow moon above
Comes a serenade of frogs
Singing out their songs of love.
Calling to each other.
Croaking,
Croaking all night long.
While a gentle sawah breeze
Filters softly through their song,
In the sawah
With a yellow moon above.

Spikelets have burst out
of the leaves. Each tiny grain is
crowned with a flower. A soft
night breeze blows from one
flower to another. In order for
the rice to develop, the plants
must share their pollen.

In the soft and misty sawah
In a quiet sawah rain,
A flock of hungry birds arrive
To drink the juicy grain.
But the people have been watching,
Waiting,
Waiting since the dawn.
And they shout
And clack
And shake
And scream
Until the birds are gone
From the sawah
Where the rain
Is soft and misty.

The plants have sprouted hundreds of little branches. On each branch are dozens of tiny green kernels. And inside each kernel is a sweet, delicious liquid that will harden into a grain of rice . . . if the birds don't drink it first.

There are mice in the sawah,
Leaping,
Squeaking,
Squealing mice.
Knocking down the healthy plants.
Ravaging the rice.
Smashing stems
And cracking kernels.
Eating as they go.
"Get out of here," the farmer calls,
Slashing with his hoe,
In the sawah
Where the rice
Is nearly ripe.

The green plants are turning golden and the rice is heavy on the stems. Soon the water will be stopped from flowing onto the fields. The sawahs must be nearly dry for the harvest.

There are people in the sawah
Cutting,
Threshing,
Picking,
Packing.
Most are working,
Some are drinking,
And a few of them are snacking.
Single file
The ants are marching,
Working where the people eat,
Picking up the bits and pieces
Of whatever food is sweet.
In the sawah
Where the ants
And people eat.

Some people cut. Some slap the plants against a slanted wooden board so that ripe kernels will fall off. Others toss the rice into the air, cleaning out bits of leaves and stems. At the end of the day, the workers put the rice into bags and then carry the bags out of the sawah on the tops of their heads.

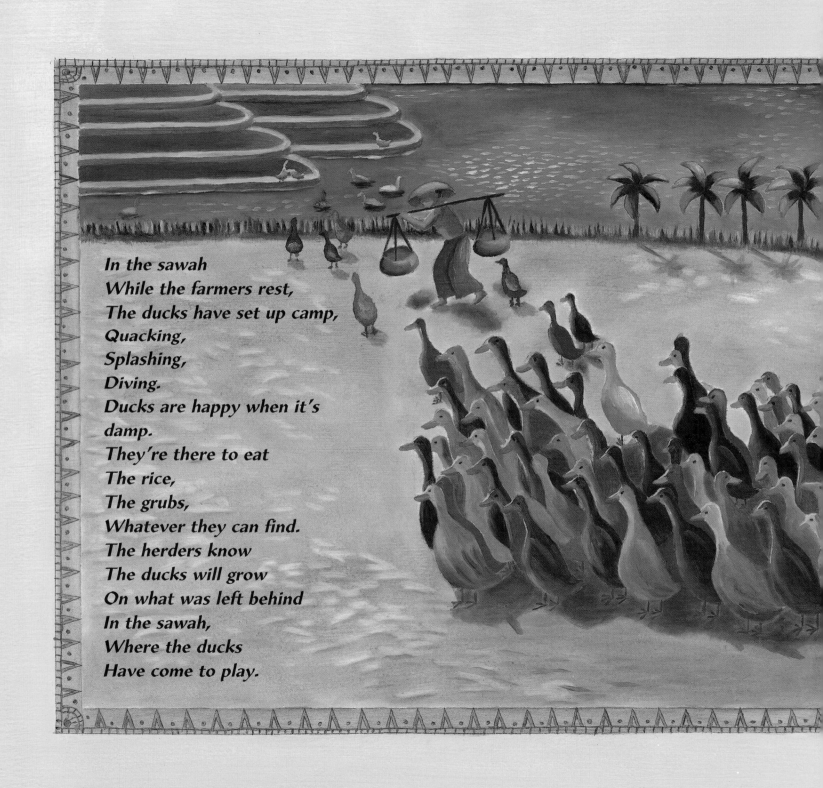

In the sawah
While the farmers rest,
The ducks have set up camp,
Quacking,
Splashing,
Diving.
Ducks are happy when it's
damp.
They're there to eat
The rice,
The grubs,
Whatever they can find.
The herders know
The ducks will grow
On what was left behind
In the sawah,
Where the ducks
Have come to play.

After the harvest, duck herders bring their ducks to the sawah. All day the ducks play and eat. Even if the herder leaves, the ducks will stay close to the herder's bamboo pole.

In the quiet of the sawah
Near the frangipani tree,
Some very special offerings
Are made to Dewi Sri.
"Thank you," says the farmer.
"Thank you," says his wife.
Then they lift their hands in prayer,
For they know that rice is life.

Dewi Sri is the goddess of rice. The farmers and their
families ask for her help when they plant the rice and for
her protection when the rice is growing. As soon as the
rice is harvested, they offer their thanks.

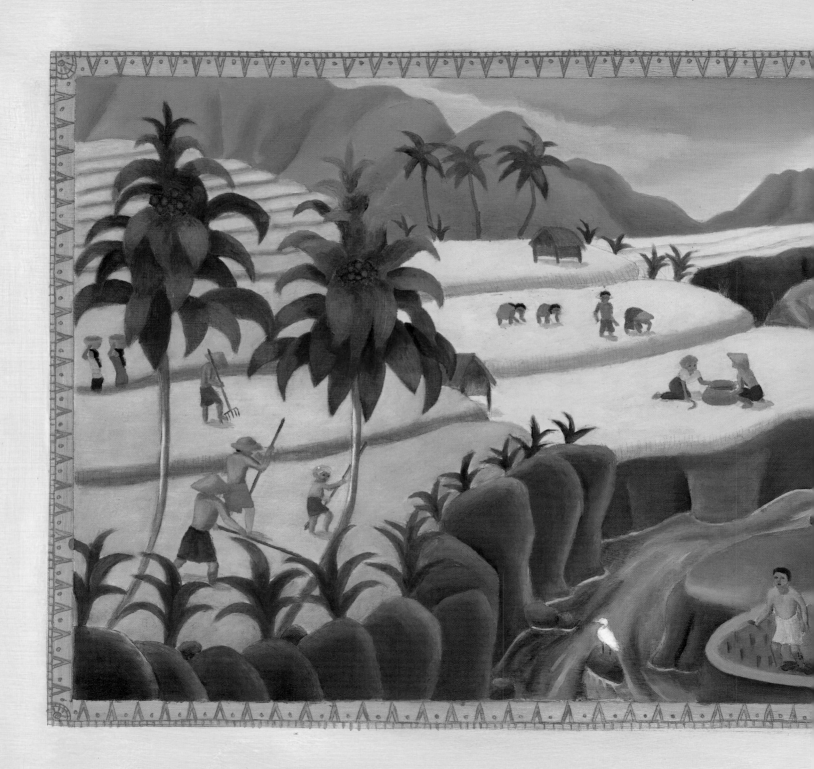

In the sawah there is quiet.
There is noise.
There is rain.

In the sawah there is sun.
There is laughter.
There is pain.
In the warm and muddy sawah
There is peace.
There is strife.

In Bali, in the sawah, there is life.